I0792027

Decline

An Appeal to We the People

ROGERIO A. DUARTE

Archway Publishing books may be ordered
through booksellers or by contacting:

Archway Publishing
1663 Liberty Drive
Bloomington, IN 47403
www.archwaypublishing.com
844-669-3957

ISBN: 978-1-6657-3295-6 (sc)
ISBN: 978-1-6657-3296-3 (e)

Library of Congress Control Number: 2022920671

Print information available on the last page.

Archway Publishing rev. date: 11/23/2022

To all those who have served, and
to all those who made the ultimate
sacrifice, so that our nation shall
not perish from the earth.

Contents

Preface

Primarily, this work is not based on scientific research, nor is it a thesis or a theory. You will find no footnotes or bibliography. What you will find is social and political commentary on the state of the American republic. What I offer are the facts and truths as I have been exposed to them. You may agree or disagree. You can always do an internet search if you doubt the veracity of my words.

Next, some may find in this work words that are beyond their vocabulary. To them I say, "Grab a dictionary or do an Internet search, and expand your vocabulary and your mind." Education and knowledge are important in life.

My education includes sociology, criminology, political science, and technology management. My life experiences include loss prevention, teaching IT technology and middle school math, and military service. I am neither a Democrat nor a Republican, nor even an outright Libertarian. I am a libertarian constitutionalist. If that confuses you, allow me to elaborate. I believe in the individual over the collective. I acknowledge that government should be limited in scope and size.

The US Constitution, as written, should be our guide when formulating public policy. It limits government to specific powers and grants all others to the people. For the record, I lean left and right depending on the circumstances and issues. I say all of this to give you an idea of where I am coming from. Mostly, it is to show you I am not just some crackpot conspiracy theorist.

I often drive for work and have a lot of time to think. The shooting in the school in Uvalde, Texas, on May 24, 2022, struck me especially hard. Not only because of the senseless violence but because of the lack of response by those who are sworn to protect the public.

This got me wondering what went wrong. And it started germinating in my mind and led to increased questions. How does society get to this point? Why would those sworn to protect and serve betray their oath in cowardice? Is there something larger at work here? Just when did thing begin to get this far out of control?

Twenty-one Americans are dead, and their families are in mourning, because the government failed to provide one of its most basic functions. And while this is not the first time there has been a mass shooting, it is one where the final carnage could have been prevented.

Over time, this morphed more into a general treatise on government and what it can and cannot do than I had originally thought. I began to save recordings of random thoughts and suddenly, one day, decided that perhaps I needed to coalesce these thoughts into a book and share it with my fellow Americans.

I proceeded to lay out my case in the spirit of Thomas Paine's *Common Sense,* listing justifications for why our government is broken. Will I achieve the same or a different result? Only you, the reader, and time, can say.

Acknowledgments

To the victims and families impacted by the school shooting in Uvalde, Texas. An unlikely muse to be sure, but the event provided the genesis for my thoughts on this literary journey.

To my mother, Patricia Duarte, for the gifts of life, a love of reading, and the value of an education.

To the Founding Fathers, for their unwavering commitment to the natural rights of humankind and their unparalleled wisdom in creating an enduring document of freedom.

To Patricia Viera Lapan, for being my first reader and a great cheerleader.

To Ginny Brown Phelps, for providing me with critical yet constructive criticism.

Introduction

The sitting president of the United States of America has stated that our democracy is under threat. He is wrong on both counts. The Founding Fathers rejected democracy as our form of government in 1789. They saw the dangers of mob rule. Additionally, when an estimated half of the electorate has different thoughts and ideas, that itself is not a threat to government but a warning that perhaps it is not following the will of the people.

Today, sadly, what we effectively have is the rule of twin mobs, not one. Democrats and Republicans are locked in a stasis of opposing thoughts with neither side willing to compromise or to (for the most part) cooperate. "We the People" have forgotten that the government serves us and not itself.

What you are about to read is my attempt to move the logjam. By highlighting some of the problems that the American republic faces and their genesis in the turmoil of the 1960s, it is my hope to make *all* people think twice about the direction we are headed in.

Reflection and public discourse are a healthy necessity for a society. However, when one group chooses to hijack the narrative and prevent said discourse, you have a recipe for disaster.

This nation, this republic, is in crisis.

Chapter 1

The Beginning of Enlightenment

It is within this framework that I have decided to muse on what exactly has gone wrong with the great experiment that is the American constitutional republic. As with many things in life, it is complicated and multifaceted. But where to begin? Perhaps with a list? In no particular order, we have the following:

- overreaching, out-of-control government
- self-serving, power-mongering politicians
- a failed war on poverty
- a failed war on drugs
- excessive criminal violence
- lack of respect for law and order
- abandonment of self-reliance and responsibility
- unchecked illegal immigration
- declining or nonexistent morals and values
- the scourge of fatherless children
- an underperforming and misguided education system
- the rise of secularism
- the assault on biology and language

- an ongoing war against the natural right of self-defense
- unnecessary sexualization of children
- political correctness and wokeness
- a mass media that is overwhelmingly polarized

Some of these started gaining traction in the early twentieth century with the beginning of the so-called "progressive" movement. Others are more recent. But the process accelerated significantly in the 1960s. Since then, the downfall of our society has continued unabated. Nearly insurmountable obstacles stand in the way of fixing the disease that has crippled us. It has many faces and allies and most often goes by multiple names, such as progressivism, leftism, socialist democracy, wokeness, and to a lesser degree, liberalism. This cancer must be countered if the long-standing and time-tested ideals of the American republic are to survive. But how? How do concerned citizens rage against the mighty juggernaut that we have allowed to grow to a point of virtual noncontainment?

By fighting back with reason, logic, common sense, and a healthy dose of belief in the Constitution of the United States of America. This offensive must happen soon, before all is utterly lost. We must counterattack from the ballot box and the jury box. And, if ultimately necessary, the cartridge box. I wish I had thought of the three-box system of rights, but I did not. Those thoughts come from the words of Frederick Douglass.

I am not a supreme wisdom, yet I do have wisdom to offer. There are those who will refute the doctrine contained herein. To them I say, "Listen to the words, take heed, and perhaps the blinders will be lifted from your eyes."

Now here is an interesting and telling exercise to determine where the heart and soul of the republic are. Look at Electoral College maps of federal elections. This tells us who voted Democrat and who voted Republican, for the most part. Now look at the same map of the United States, but one broken down by county. You will see a remarkably interesting pattern. For the most part, Democratic voters are centered in large, urban areas.

Interestingly, if you wonder why a state voted one way instead of another, take a look at the county election map. Georgia and Pennsylvania are stark representations of this. A vast majority of the states vote conservatively; the liberal votes come from the big, urban areas in those states.

Having seen this, it is hard for me to believe that the majority of Americans are liberal and progressive in nature. Numerically, the suggestion has merit, of course. But when faced with this reality, I have to believe in my heart that the majority of Americans are not in line with changing the nature of the values of this great republic just for the sake of change.

It would seem that for some reason, history has decided that great nations and empires can only endure for two hundred to three hundred years. We find ourselves at this precipice with the coming of our 250th anniversary of independence. The America I know and love cannot continue to endure the current erosion of faculty, spirit, and freedom that was bequeathed to us by our forebears. Many of us will take up the mantle to challenge this calling, but many others will continue to pay lip service to our precipitous slide into obscurity. How some can revel in this mediocrity is beyond the capability of my reasoning to understand. It is for the latter that these words are intended. All of us should not want this great experiment to be callously tossed aside in the name of expediency and indulgence.

Now although the Declaration of Independence is not an official part of our governmental structure, it is a guidebook for it. The words written after the preamble, in my opinion, are the most important.

> That to secure these right
> Governments are instituted
> among Men, deriving their just
> powers from the consent of the
> governed. That whenever any
> Form of Government becomes
> destructive of these ends, it is
> the Right of the People to alter
> or to abolish it, and to institute
> new Government, laying its
> foundation on such principles

and organizing its powers in such form, as to them shall seem most likely to affect their Safety and Happiness.

Basically, any time "We the People" decide that the government isn't working properly or within its bounds, then "We the People" can, and should, either fix it or tear it down and start over again as we see fit. I would be remiss if I did not state that I am not a huge fan of starting over. I believe we do not have thinkers of the caliber of the Founding Fathers. Too much can go wrong. I am a proponent of altering the government. Of putting it back in the cage that was constructed to limit it in the first place.

Societies in general are founded on two types of law; this should be understood so that a basic foundation of debate and conversation can be established. The types of law are moral law and civil law.

Moral law is the one lacking in many societies, especially those based on Marxist thought. It is founded in basic human rights, the agreed upon natural rights that exist outside of, and without, government presence or consent. Some religions have codified some moral law, such as the Christian Ten Commandments. But morals do not depend on religion to exist. Interestingly, some will argue exactly what is meant by "basic" human rights. In essence, they are the right to live, to defend yourself from harm, to seek out opportunity, and to coexist with whom you choose. The United Nations has greatly expanded this list, but I do not agree with their interpretations of basic human rights.

Civil law is created by government to enforce rules of behavior as well as moral law. We do not go around simply murdering one another. Why? Because first, it is a moral law not to. And second, it has been codified that this is the way we expect members of a society to behave for the betterment of said society. These laws are punitive in nature and carry penalties for violating them. The penalties are there to ensure compliance and deter criminal activity.

As a society, we look to these two types of laws for self-regulation. We have the freedom to choose to follow/obey them or to ignore/

disobey them. But they are a necessary part of society to function in a civilized manner so that we can respect one another and go about our lives in general peace.

Once we have organized into a society and decided upon the need for a government, we must lay the groundwork for what that government can and cannot do. We need methods in place to redress grievances, whether they be with others or with the government itself. We also need a methodology for all this to work in concert to manage the system we have put in place. This is a generalization of what it takes to make a nation and is intended as a primer for the rest of my work.

I would like to mention that I think it is amazing how many people and organizations are suddenly concerned with threats to our democracy. We are not a democracy; we are a constitutional republic that holds democratic elections. This point cannot be emphasized enough. Ignorance is a disease, not bliss. While it can be argued that there are some threats to our republic, the truth is that these are really threats. They are threats to their control of power over "We the People." That is what they are concerned. They fear that we will finally find the courage and the voice to call them on their lies and manipulation and demand redress.

Chapter 2

The Present State
of the Republic

The annual tradition of the State of the Union address has, in the last handful of decades, become largely scripted political theater. Therefore, I offer to you the State of the Republic in its place.

We are quite polarized on a number of issues, and this sentiment is exacerbated by the entrenched two-party political system. Left versus right. Liberal versus conservative. Democrat versus Republican. The nation is adrift and as stuck as Odysseus was between the Scylla and Charybdis. Virtually no one wants to budge from their viewpoint. Once you begin to look into each of these microcosms, it becomes clearer as to why.

There are those who believe that our nation is rotten to the core, that it was founded racist, classist, and sexist. Critical race theory points to skin color as the most important factor in society. Its proponents are pushing to have it taught at the elementary level of education, which is not where issues requiring critical thinking skills should be taught.

Add to this Black Lives Matter. And yes, they do. But then again so do all lives. BLM was begun by self-described Marxists. The majority of the money raised has not reached the black communities. What is their true purpose? To tear down the social fabric of America and make it more acceptable to socialism.

Social justice warriors are their staunch allies. They preach diversity, inclusivity, and equity in every facet of life without regard for the consequences. This decidedly un-American way of thinking has morphed and spread with the rise of things, such as wokeness and cancel culture. Respect for differing opinions has been replaced with deference only to their opinions.

For those who are not sure what being woke is, I offer this brilliant definition for woke that I came across on the internet. I feel the need to share it here.

> It is a state of awareness achieved only by those stupid enough to find injustice in everything except their own behavior.

Having identified the actors in this area of thought, we can move on to more substantive aspects of it. The struggle for nontraditional lifestyles and identities is not something to be dismissed. We all have the individual right to be free. However, when you begin indoctrinating children as young as five years old by bringing them to gay bars and drag queen reading time, you have perhaps gone too far.

These social forces, coupled with the preparation of children in grades K–12 and their indoctrination at the collegiate level, are vying to completely redefine the republic. Most people are amicable to new ideas and perceptions. It is when those are forcefully fed to the public that people resist and become adversarial. Many parents, for example, do not take very kindly to being told how their children should be raised.

Politically, we have the quagmire of the power-hungry, corruptible, two-party system. It is a system that puts one side against the other to meet its own ends and a system that does not always affect constitutional legislation. Many look to the government for solutions to problems. Sadly, they more often make the problem worse (Iraq and Afghanistan) or—better yet—throw endless money at a problem with no appreciable affect (war on poverty and war on drugs). It has often been said that the scariest words in the English language are "I'm from the government and I am here to help."

Immigration is a mess. We have a system in place to allow for it to happen lawfully. Yet many decide to just vote with their feet and invade (yes, invade, for what else do you call unlawful entry?) the country like swarms of locusts descending on the fields. Cities offer sanctuary and even legal documents to illegal immigrants. But this fits the transformation of America agenda so nothing gets done.

Our military is continually called upon not just to break things and kill enemies but to nation build, which is not their purview or forte. Once a bastion of will against the social forces and tides of our society, it too has succumbed to the woke style of thinking.

Our so-called leaders (lest we forget that they are just representatives) continually lie and manipulate words to keep the votes and keep their fiefdoms intact. And there is no unified outrage at these shameless acts of snake oil salesmanship. We even have those who believe the election system is being outright manipulated and rigged. They spur on rioters and call them protestors while they label protestors as insurrectionists.

> Ours may become the first civilization destroyed, not by the power of our enemies, but by the ignorance of our teachers and the dangerous nonsense they are teaching our children. In an age of artificial intelligence, they are creating artificial stupidity. (Thomas Sowell)

Education in my home state has some downright stupid ideas. Much of it is focused on the standardized tests that are given to students toward the end of every year. And that is one of the problems. The English test is taken in March and the math test is taken in May. The curriculum imposed by the state legislature requires a teacher to educate the students on it. How is an English teacher supposed to get 180 days of teaching in before March? And what do they do after that? Same thing goes for the math teacher. They have a little more time than the English teacher but still need to cram the curriculum into a smaller space than they are given. Science and history are included, with the latter being almost an afterthought.

I know this from my personal experience, having taught middle school mathematics for nine years. One of the most troubling things I ever read in my research for my required education as a teacher is that "the math curriculum in the United States is a mile wide and an inch deep." What this means is we teach a whole lot of subjects but very rarely to any depth of knowledge. This is a major problem because repetition is a major component in learning and retaining information. Add to this the fact that, as aforementioned, you do not have enough time to teach everything, and you have a problem. Besides, let us be honest. How many of you have ever had a need for the Pythagorean theorem in your lives? Yet we all learn it.

There is nothing wrong with standardized testing; there is nothing wrong with ensuring that the curriculum is being taught. However, there is a problem with the current system, and I use this as an example for it may very well be the same elsewhere. Standardized tests in middle and high school levels of education should be administered during the last two weeks of the school year. They should be counted as finals. This would give teachers the maximum amount of time to pass on the curriculum and hopefully have their students retain it. And retention is the core of learning and understanding.

But then you have the problem that even though 180 days are assigned, rarely do you get them. Yes, snow days do affect some school year lengths in some locations, but I am not talking about that. I am referring to the explosion of so-called half days. Often these are days carved out of the curriculum whereby students go to school for a few hours, get no meaningful education during those few hours, and then their teachers gather together to do *professional development*, which is just a euphemism for wasteful hyperbole. Now keep in mind I was not educated to be an educator. (How ridiculous is that concept?) I fell into the position quite by accident.

Although I was a licensed educator, I was

never fully accepted by most of my peers. Because I did not learn to teach the way they learned to teach. And quite often I found that their methods did not work or did not work as well as my basic method. Students want to know one thing: how. How do I solve this math problem? How do I do this experiment in science? How do I understand the main subject of a story? That is all they want, yet we give them many other things that just cloud and confuse their minds.

The focus on more critical thinking is an admirable one, but it is being done at the cost of another excellent element of education: memorization. There is nothing wrong with rote memorization, especially in certain subject areas, but the elites and teachers' unions feel differently. In eighth grade, I had a math teacher who forced us every week to do a quiz on fraction to decimal to percent conversions. He told us this would be extremely helpful for us later on in high school and in life. We did not question him. We studied and took the quizzes and got our grades. It was not long before I found he was right and it was helpful to know that, for example, one-sixth is .167, rounded off the repeating decimal. I did the same with my students and some complained. Most accepted it, and I can only hope that it helped them as it helped me. But enough on the state of education.

One aspect of the enemy of common sense and the proper way this republic should run is that they rely on the gray area of things to accomplish their goals. You see, with a gray area, there is room for movement, realigning, and modification. But this takes out the element of black and white. Some things are just black and white, and there is some benefit to seeing a gray area with respect to some occurrences. However, with the concept of good and evil, it is very wasteful and repugnant.

The problem is too many people do not delineate between good and evil anymore. It used to be that if someone committed a crime and was found guilty, they would be punished and sentenced to jail time. Now we are more lenient and allow for the gray area to cloud our judgment and give people parole instead. Or if they are already in prison, we give them time off for good behavior. This flies in the face of the very concept of fighting evil with good.

You see, the gray area provides wiggle room; it is not so absolute. This is why leftists and progressives like to describe the Constitution of the United States as a living and breathing document that should change with the times. I vehemently disagree with this assessment. The Constitution stands the test of time and has a mechanism in place for amending it. It says what it says and means what it means. It is this lackadaisical attitude that has helped to contribute to many of our problems since the 1960s.

A brief word on hatred. I do not hate Marxists, leftists, and progressives. Hate is an extraordinarily strong emotion that should be reserved for the direst circumstances. I do think they are stupid and ignorant all at the same time. But only by educating them can we show them the damage they have done and will do to the republic. There is enough hatred to go around with our polarized political system. We need to move beyond this metaphorical rut we find ourselves in if we are to correct the course we are on.

The Constitution provides us with a framework in which to posit our laws and regulations.

The Founding Fathers, who were not misogynistic or bigoted as some will have you believe, were wise enough to separate the fact that issues of national importance should be governed by the national Constitution while issues of social importance should be governed by the states. They gambled on a radical new form of government, and it paid off for almost two hundred years. Until the 1960s.

Where does the Constitution state that the government should pay people not to work? Where does it state the government can ignore it and develop laws that are against it? Where does it say that we are all entitled to an equality of outcomes? Most of the powers the government has now have been given to it by the leftist, progressive fools who advance an agenda to tear down and deconstruct what is the greatest nation this planet has ever seen.

The media and journalists used to be trusted to be honest, straightforward, and unbiased. But that is no longer true. The vast majority of them lean left. They have for decades. And it is still moving farther left as I type this. It spawned a reaction from the right to get their message out and heard. And now they lob insults at one another in bitter, partisan bickering.

In no other topic is this more obvious than that of gun ownership and the Second Amendment. Whether you like it or not, and even if you do not understand the construction of the language of it, it gives the right to own a gun to the people. Some argue there are reasonable controls to be imposed while others say, "What part of 'shall not be infringed' do not you understand?" The Supreme Court has ruled, correctly, that a right to self-defense exists and is applied through the Second Amendment, be it defense against a rapist, a thief, or a tyrannical government.

If my time in the military taught me anything, it was the value of a firearm for defense. Whether that comes against foreign aggression, an oppressive domestic government, or on the street against one who would do you harm, it is a lesson that too many people have not learned or refuse to learn. When did "We the People" begin to acquiesce our natural right to self-defense to the idea that the government would protect us? In the 1950s, children used to take their rifles to school and were taught how to shoot them. Then came the 1960s. A lot changed with the assassination of JFK and the shooting from the tower in Texas.

There are three instances in which murder can be lawfully justified. In an act of self-defense, when applying the death penalty as a punishment for egregious crimes, and when a woman decides to abort a baby. The first often requires a firearm, especially for women, to be an equalizer. The second has many checks and balances to ensure that the guilt of the perpetrator is true enough so that they are not put to death by accident. The last one is a touchy subject, especially with the Supreme Court overturning the ruling of Roe v. Wade. The court acted in the interest of the Constitution itself in reversing an earlier decision that was erroneously applied. It is a social issue and is therefore now back in the hands of state governments, were the Founding Fathers intended such issues to be.

Now a legal right to self-defense does not give one the right to break the law. Mass shootings and gangland murders are still against the laws of a civil society. Everyone should understand this fact. Yet what do the politicians do? They rail with pomp and circumstance to turn tragedies into opportunities for their agenda. Instead of enforcing existing laws and punishing the guilty, they seek to enact laws that further erode the inalienable, natural rights of the people to keep and bear arms. In case you missed it, the US Supreme Court has ruled in the past that the police have no duty to protect you, the individual, only the public as a whole. If this is the case, then who but you are responsible for your own safety and protection?

The dreaded AR-15. You would think this was the devil's sword the way it is described. Allow me to educate your ignorance (or blatant stupidity). The Armalite Rifle (hence, AR) designated "15" is semiautomatic. Pull the trigger, and one bullet comes out of the barrel. It is not a military weapon and is incapable of fully automatic fire (unless you violate the law and illegally convert it to do such). It is no more a *weapon of war* than any other semiautomatic rifle. Do yourself a favor: internet search an image of the M1 rifle and the AR-15 rifle. Compare them visually. Both operate the same basic way. Yet one should be banned because it looks scary. This is the willful ignorance of most of our elected *representatives*.

How do we meet our future energy needs? Do we rush headlong into the green energy revolution, or do we take a more intelligent path of phased diversity? Solar and wind are great resources of renewable energy. However, they are not sustainable without the use of batteries. They only produce when those resources are present.

We need to embrace several technologies to make the goal of clean energy a reality. Solar and wind, yes. But also tidal, geothermal, hydro, and nuclear.

Yes nuclear. New technology makes reactors safer and smaller than previously manufactured ones. And the holy grail of power, nuclear fusion, is close to being developed. Safer and cleaner than nuclear fission, this is the key to a renewable energy future. It can sustain energy needs during periods when other renewable sources of energy aren't producing.

Electric vehicles are the new rage. They bear the same problem as wind and solar. They rely on batteries. Without going into pros and cons, let it be said that the Achilles' heel is the need for a battery. Developing alternative methods of powering vehicles, such as using hydrogen, make more sense in the long run.

We do not need a Green New Deal. What we need is a national, sustained effort to evolve fusion and hydrogen technology. It took us about nine years to put men on the moon. That kind of effort is what we need right now to take us into a cleaner future.

So what are we left with? A maelstrom of negativity that the media gladly and willfully stirs up. How do we get out of this funk and go back to a time when America was respected by "We the People"? The solution is to start in the most obvious place and alter our government, deconstruct the two-party system, and return it to the days when it worked for the people and not against them.

Chapter 3

The Bloated Leviathan of Government

★ ★ ★ ★

Politicians are like diapers. They need to be changed often, and for the same reason. I didn't write that, but I find it very accurate and worth repeating. Also, keep in mind my definition of the word *politics* breaks down into two words: *poly,* meaning many, and *ticks,* meaning bloodsucking creatures.

The rights of humankind exist without government. The Founding Fathers knew this truth to be fact. Government is only instituted by a society to provide some semblance of order and reason and to institute laws from which civility can be derived. Indulgence in whims and fads may be socially acceptable, but they are no way to structure a just and orderly republic. There are enough challenges in the world for our great nation without conjuring up others that we have the ability to deny. We owe this much to our forebears and our posterity.

I see a political spectrum that has, in my lifetime, shifted to the left. That is to say the entire spectrum is sliding in that direction. Democrats have become increasingly leftist in their thoughts and actions. Republicans seem to be more moderate than they have been in the past. Progressive is so far off the chart to the left that a new border had to be drawn, while conservatives hold fast to maintaining their border on the right, causing a stretching affect between them and the middle.

Governments are instituted by people to service them and not the other way around. Many have seemed to forget that the government exists at the whim of the people and that we elect representatives to carry out said will. Unfortunately, self-serving and self-righteous individuals are elected by the unthinking populace. Redress of grievances therefore becomes nearly impossible when those we elect forget their place.

In the words of the singer/songwriter Sting, there is no monopoly in common sense on either side of the political fence. Those words were written in the 1980s toward the end of the Cold War struggle against Soviet communism. However, they do apply to other instances and are very telling about the current political landscape in the republic.

In nature, nothing is owed to you. Nature is where we derive our natural rights from. Therefore, for the vast majority of us, we earn what we work for. There are no handouts, no free rides, and no concept of so-called universal basic income. Government should not exist to do these things. It should exist to secure the natural rights of man and to ensure that the wall of home within the framework of the Constitution.

Different generations of people always have different views, but it seems the gaps between generations have been growing wider and wider as time passes from the Greatest Generation to Generation Z. What seems to be a core problem is that the majority of the people have forgotten that our Constitution defines our freedoms that preexist government, are inalienable, and are the natural rights of humankind.

With those thoughts in mind, the grossly non-Republican systems of government need to be challenged and reversed. No, I am not talking about the Republican Party. I am referring to the ideal of Republicanism. It was espoused and practiced by none other than George Washington himself. He didn't seek power. He served when called and only at the whim of the people. Yet when they clamored for more, he resisted the call to glory, having done his civic duty.

Washington was also a strong opponent of political parties and warned us against them. Apparently, we didn't listen. To paraphrase Thomas Paine,

> let the names of democrat and republican be extinct. Let none other be heard among us than those of a good citizen and a virtuous supporter of the rights of mankind for the Republic of the United States of America.

A return to civil service and the elimination of politics as a career is the best place to start. Term limits should be in place to prevent the coalescence of power and greed. Incumbents should be challenged, for they hold a power card in the game. Replace exorbitant salaries and perks with simple travel and service stipends. And let them have the same medical insurance as the people have. Public service was and should once again become a calling, not an occupation.

Rational, logical, and sensible discussion and debate should be at the core of every decision made by government. It rarely is. Agendas, pork barrel projects, and backroom deals are the way it is done. And unless we vote the corrupt out or use the courts to nullify their unlawful positions, we are left with only one alternative to enforce change: the taking up of arms.

Now you perhaps see why they want to limit guns in the hands of the people. Ask the Jews in Germany in the 1930s how that went for them. And while you're at it, ask why the Gun Control Act of 1968 was pattered nearly directly from the Nazi Weapons Law of 1934. Yeah, scary, isn't it?

I love my country, but I am sick to death about its government. I am not an anarchist. I am a pragmatist. Our Declaration of Independence speaks to the fact that when we no longer agree with our government, we have the rights to readdress grievances and replace that government. The unfortunate thing is that our enemies are trying to do the same thing for all the wrong reasons. It is incumbent upon us, the people, to rise up and stand up for what is right, good, and just.

Is our nation infallible? Not at all. But it is the last, best hope for individual freedom in this entire world. Should our constitutional republic become extinct and replaced by another form of government that is not of the people, by the people, and for the people, then all is truly lost.

While we are on the subject of government, it should be noted that its scope and size are not only grotesque but also unmanageable. Many of these offices and departments are unconstitutional and should be eliminated. Nothing should exist that does not meet the primary functioning of government as defined by the Constitution (as amended).

Originally, the federal government had four departments. Although their names have changed over time, those departments still exist today. They are the Department of Defense, Department of State, Department of Justice, and Department of the Treasury. These executive departments were constructed to help the fledgling federal government carry out its duties and obligations. As the federal government expanded, more departments were added. At this time, there are now fifteen executive departments under the federal government. And dozens more offices under each of those. This bloating of the system has often been described as necessary. Some believe that the government can solve problems and can do some good in some areas. I am of the opposite belief. The federal government, as overburdened and large as it is, is an ineffective mechanism to get anything done. Well, I shouldn't say "anything." There are some things that we still do at a federal level that are effective. But most of the tasks carried out by these executive departments are wasteful in both time and money. Here's the rundown:

- US Department of Agriculture
- US Department of Commerce
- US Department of Defense
- US Department of Education
- US Department of Energy
- US Department of Health and Human Services
- US Department of Homeland Security
- US Department of Housing and Urban Development

- US Department of Justice
- US Department of Labor
- US Department of State
- US Department of the Interior
- US Department of the Treasury
- US Department of Transportation
- US Department of Veterans Affairs

There are some necessities in life (air, water, food, shelter, etc.) and necessary evils (laundry, taxes, etc.). The necessary evils I want to discuss. They should be limited to what is absolutely required to meet the needs of what government is supposed to provide. We have unfortunately gone way overboard in what is supposed to be provided, and it has required a parallel increase in taxation. This is not sustainable and has led to record-breaking, insane levels of debt.

The primary target is the IRS, within the Treasury. Not only is our income tax system a labyrinthine mess, but it is also patently unjust and unfair. It punishes hard work, drive, and ambition by charging more tax the more you make. The IRS should be eliminated, the tax code should be abolished, and a better system such as the fair tax should be put in its place. Do not let one political party claim that higher taxes in the current system is somehow fair. It most assuredly is not. It is a scam to fatten governmental coffers to pay out favors in the form of laws enacted. No more tax shelters, tax dodging, filings, or audits, and you get to keep your whole paycheck!

Next to go is the so-called Department of Education. The failure of this endeavor should be clear to all. It has succeeded in indoctrinating our youth over several generations to accept the government as parent and savior. It has quashed individualism at the expense of the collective "good." It has championed the idea that certain people are victims.

Marxism and leftism run rampant in most universities. The goal is to convert the masses to their belief system until any thoughts that do not align with those of their dogma is silenced or cowed into submission. The majority of college-age students have been brainwashed into believing that the communist ideology (which is responsible for at least 100 million deaths in the twentieth century) is a good idea! The evidence is plain to see for anyone in the present day what is going on in higher learning.

Oh, and while I'm at it, let's get rid of the idea that you need a college degree. End federal financial aid and continue to take in payments for the legally binding contracts on the funds you have availed yourself of. As for myself, I've never missed a payment, and unfortunately, I racked up a princely sum in loans I will be paying until I die because I bought into the big lie. Degrees are necessary for some occupations, but not most. Do yourself a favor. Learn a trade or invest yourself in an internship.

Anecdotes are generally unreliable, but sometimes they are very poignant. I will give you one such anecdote. In my junior year introduction to criminology class, the teacher posited a situation to us and had us break up into groups to discuss it. The gist of what was presented was that a wall guard in East Berlin shot and killed someone trying to escape. Ten years later with the reunification of Germany, they put this man on trial for murder. As I was trying to reason out potential explanations as to how the person was shot (apparently the guard claimed to fire a warning shot and was not trying to actually shoot the person), the student in front of me blurted out, "I just wish there were no guns in the world anyways." I said to her, "You live in a pretty idealistic world, do you not?" She looked at me dumbfounded and weakly said, "What do you mean by that?" This is the education system that has fostered a junior in college who does not know what I meant. And to follow up on that, a few days later, I was speaking to one of my black professors about the incident. He asked if the girl was white. I said no. He then closed the door to his office and told me that affirmative action is the worst thing to ever happen to the country. Yes, these are only anecdotes, but they are very telling about the cancer that is eating away at the soul of our nation.

Many agencies within these US departments need to be overhauled and streamlined.

On to a hot topic: illegal immigration.

Most of us here today are children of immigrants. My mother was born in California, and my father on Faial, an island of the Azores chain. I am a first-generation American in my family. Many others have similar stories. When someone talks about illegal immigration, they are referring to those who willfully enters the US without permission. Sure, some say humans aren't illegal, but their actions can be. Sneaking into the country is akin to trespassing in a house. You know you do not belong there, yet there you are. And once you avail yourself of the goods and services presented by misguided fools, you've just graduated to burglary. Not to mention you are spitting in the face of everyone who has ever legally immigrated here, and their posterity, as well as those currently waiting. Yet the problem persists. To hell with obeying the law, right? Only suckers and fools follow the law.

Speaking of the law, since when does any government have the right or responsibility to provide any wage to a citizen, let alone a *living wage?* The first minimum wage law at the federal level was passed in 1938. A capitalist economy, which we have, consists of private citizens and private businesses. When one seeks employment, one either accepts what is offered or negotiate. That is the nature of things. Anything else is essentially socialism.

With one fell swoop, let's eliminate the departments, or reconstruct agencies, which effectively do nothing that Congress cannot do by passing constitutional laws. Goodbye to Agriculture, Commerce, Education, Housing and Urban Development, Labor, and Transportation. Next, fold Homeland Security and Veterans Affairs into Defense. Likewise, fold Energy and Health and Human Services into Interior. Perhaps even rename it Homeland? There, down to a manageable five departments, Interior being the only addition to remain above the original four.

The point should be clear. Government is not the solution; it is, in its current state, the problem. Balance the budget; do not spend more than you earn. Pay off your debts. Do what the people do.

We need to remove the shackles the government has placed on "We the People" over time and go back to a simpler place in our history, where the government actually worked for us instead of against us.

> Nobody has a more sacred obligation to obey the law than those who make the laws. (Jean Anouilh)

Chapter 4

The National Suicide of Morality and Ethics

★ ★ ★ ★

According to Malcolm X,

> When the people who are in power want to justify something that is bad, they use the press. And they'll use the press to create a humanitarian image, for a devil, or a devil image for a humanitarian. They'll take a person who's the victim of a crime, and make it appear he's the criminal, and they'll take the criminal and make it appear he's the victim of the crime.

Is it any wonder why there is rampant disrespect for law and order? This is but the tip of the iceberg. With some periods of exception, crime has steadily risen since the 1960s. What changed to make crime so popular? What occurred to make your neighbors celebrate anarchy and lawlessness? Why do we as a society tolerate it? Criminals should be punished. Period.

Sometimes, we rightfully decide that something should no longer be a crime.

Decriminalization of marijuana comes to mind. It never should have been a crime. *What gives government the right to outlaw something that grows in the ground?* The war on drugs is an abject failure. Drugs are still available, more lethal ones even, and billions of dollars have been wasted. Legalize cocaine and opium, tax them, and use the revenue, in part, to support addiction/education programs and largely to pay down the unbearable national debt. Not a popular idea, I know!

But nowhere is lawlessness seen more clearly than in large cities. Cities where the war on poverty has raged since the mid-1960s. It is yet another war we lost. Yet like insane robots, we keep throwing more money at welfare and social programs, expecting that someday it will pay off. It never will.

Couple this with a sad but significant increase in children born to fatherless families, and your recipe for disaster is complete. Those children have a higher likelihood of being a dropout from school and/or being involved in gangs or crime. History is supposed to teach us what to avoid and learn from it. Yet here we go again, repeating the same mistakes.

And sadly, some problems are harder to solve than others.

The decline of morality certainly plays into this picture. Decline? Free fall is more accurate. Now do not think I'm some high and mighty religious zealot. I'm not. I was raised Catholic. Then I left and found my own way and belief system. I am not a fan of organized religion, but I firmly believe in the freedom to have, and express, whatever religion you choose that does not advocate violence or human sacrifice. It just seems funny to me that the more and more secular society becomes, the more and more it descends into decadence.

When did this shift begin? Right about the 1960s. Surprised? You shouldn't be. Morals and morality are a tough call to make sometimes. But there are universal constants. Do not kill out of anger or spite. Obey the law. Respect one another. Do not cheat on your spouse. Do not misrepresent yourself or lie. It is almost as if some religion already thought of a formula for society! The further we stray from some kind of focus on mores and values, the deeper we slide into the abyss.

And what has happened to personal responsibility and self-reliance? They have been sacrificed in the name of a realignment of our society, whose aim is to destroy everything that has come before it so that a liberal, leftist utopia can be born. Once upon a time, people had these virtues and lived their lives accordingly. There was a sense of ethics: getting up in the morning, going to work, and putting in a day's labor to earn the money to do what you wanted to do with your life. That vision has been eroded and worn away over time by those who would have you believe that you are a fool for following such a path. Why work hard when you can just sit at home and let the government take care of you? Sadly, many of fallen under the spell of the welfare state and surrendered themselves to the ideals of the left. Only by standing strong and reaffirming those beliefs can we begin to take back the narrative and succeed in turning the decline of this republic around.

We have those decrying that religion is for fools, yet others follow the religion of secularism and claim it is just. We have a government that cannot govern effectively because too many of its representatives are worried about their own skins rather than those of their constituents. And that same government then prints trillions of dollars out of thin air in an effort to appease the masses with chaos. This of course has led us into the greatest period of economic strife that I have experienced in my lifetime on this planet. One group preaches that the rich are to blame, another that it is corporate greed, and yet another (our very own government) that is the result of a foreign power invading its neighboring state. We only have ourselves to blame for the state of things because we apparently keep electing the same imbeciles into office who do not solve our problems.

Intolerance is in their minds; the opposition seeks to have the moral imperative. Yes, the irony of the situation is that they do not. In fact, it can be claimed that no one does. Morality is in the heart of the beholder for certain truths. The shift toward secularism and accepting the government as savior has done nothing except to erode the human condition.

Human beings can only be one of two things, per science and biology, with very rare exception. If you are unhappy with yourself, then seek professional assistance to deal with that mental issue. Stop trying to make it all about you at the expense of mostly everyone else. It does not matter to most people who or what you are to yourself. But the majority see what their eyes tell them and comprehend what their brains tell them to make their rational decisions.

Since the beginning of human history, the science of biology has dictated that a person is either male or female unless you are an extremely rare genetic anomaly born with both sets of genitalia or none. Now you can swap your genitalia and take hormones to incite other changes, but that does not change the scientific fact that you have either XX or XY chromosomes.

A male (men) has XY chromosomes in their genotype, has nonlactating breasts, has no uterus, and has a penis and scrotum that produces sperm. A female (woman) has an XX chromosome genotype, has lactating breasts, has a uterus, has a vagina, and menstruates. Even the bones of the long-dead people tell the tale of whether they are male or female. Yet we are expected to comply with the wishes of the insane transgender movement and ignore science that has been established for millennia. Their agenda is clear: tear down all that has been and remake it as they see fit.

Now as for gender, that used to be simple. Female was assigned the gender of woman and male was assigned the gender of man. Not so much anymore. As part of their continuing goal of change, the enemies of the republic seek to revamp the English language.

You can look up a definition of gender. They all now say it is either of the two sexes, but they add that it is both a social and cultural construct rather than a biological one. And that it can change. I disagree because I grabbed a dictionary printed in 1995 and it defines gender as

> a classification corresponding to
> the two sexes and sexlessness,
> a grouping of words in some
> languages according to this as
> masculine, feminine and neuter,
> a person's sex.

Therefore, I am willing to concede as there are three genders, based on this definition. I would even go so far as to say there are actually four genders, including the genetic mutation of those who have both sets of genitalia (so-called hermaphrodites). However, I will not acceptthe fantastical delusions of people who have created their own gender based on their own self-reflection. Wanting something to be the truth does not automatically make it so.

Something like 1.4 percent of baby boomers identify as transgender. Gen Z has a roughly 20 percent rate of identification. This poses a serious question of "Why?" And it is a question we all should have the freedom to ask. Is this a natural progression of humanity? Is there something else in play causing these skyrocketing numbers? The problem is that if you ask questions, you are immediately labeled transphobic. They do not want a narrative exchange; they only want acquiescence to their beliefs. That is a disturbing circumstance.

Homosexuality was once a form of social deviance. As time has passed and certain forces have come into play, that opinion has changed, though it has not been completely erased. Nor will it ever be. Social crusaders and their supporters speak to establish this change for other classes of society. I have no issue with this, other than the fact that rather than asking for social change, it is being virtually forced down the throats of the people.

I have no qualms with, nor animosity toward, homosexuality, or transgenderism. My complaint lies in the fact that to make the changes that some see as necessary, they are employing tactics that are not in line with the vast majority of morals and values. These people decry their belief that those who do not except their ideas are Nazis or fascists. Yet they attempt to coerce society to fall in line with their viewpoint. I would say the irony is delicious, but it is rather bitter in fact.

It is important to denote the difference between deviance and being deviant. In sociological terms, deviance is expressed as anything that is outside the norm. For example, homosexuality, atheism, and anarchy exist outside the normal range of views in any given society. I acknowledge there is a variance given the particular society in question, but nonetheless, these are sociologically deviant. It does not mean a homosexual, an atheist, or an anarchist is deviant. I reserve that word more for individuals, such as pedophiles and murderers. The colloquial definition of *deviant,* and the sociological one, are not in line. And that is an important distinction to make.

There are of course extenuating circumstances and occurrences that must be acknowledged when dealing with social change and control. Suicides among people who do not feel they are within the norm are an area that needs to be explored further and needs to have more mental health resources devoted to it. This does not negate sociological fact, but it does give one pause for concern and reflection.

Our decline is artificial in nature. It has been brought about by forces that despise individuality, freedom, and natural rights. Since it is artificial, it can be reversed. But this can only take place if the people are up to the task of doing so.

> The price good men pay for indifference to public affairs is to be ruled by evil men. (Plato)

Chapter 5

The Blight
of Progressive
Liberal and
Leftist Thought

★ ★ ★ ★

"Deviance and Social Control" was the name of a course I took at Bridgewater State College circa 1994. In her introduction, the instructor stated, "If you're conservative, you do not belong here." I immediately raised my hand and said, "Why? Are there no conservative sociologists and criminologists? I can name three off the top of my head." She ignored my question and continued with her monologue, setting the tone for the rest of the semester. This course became my only C in my undergraduate studies!

Brainwashing is an essential element of control over the population of a society. It is not something that is immediate; it can be slow and take time. The progressive, leftist, liberal elements in the republic have been at it for half a century or more and have largely succeeded in winning the hearts and minds of people, especially the youth. They seek to impose and silence rather than engage in creative and constructive dialogue.

Thoughts and feelings now seem to be more important than logic and reason. The big push in the social sphere to normalize behaviors and morals that were once ridiculed or looked down upon is in full swing now. This is all being done in the names of diversity, equity, and inclusiveness. The prevailing thought is that by changing our perception of the English language, and our lack of moral ambiguity, everyone will be happier and no one will be excluded. Human nature and history show us that this is a fallacy of utopian proportions.

I distinctly recall when I believe political correctness came to the forefront on the national scene. In 1988 I went to the United Kingdom as part of my military service. I came back in 1992. It seems to me the country changed in that brief amount of time. Those who advanced the process of political correctness had succeeded in changing the national narrative. Add to this the current environment of wokeness that is running rampant, and we have an extremely serious problem to deal with. The supporters of these ideals would have you believe that this is for the better. That it is wrong to criticize someone and it is not nice to be open and truthful with someone. That *their* truth (not *the* truth) should be paramount. Statues must be torn down, and people must be essentially forced to accept that this nation was not born in glory and freedom but in racism and bigotry.

If the United States has an original sin, it is definitely slavery. It is a lesson we learned harshly, at least some of us have. Others cling to the past and insist that they are still facing the same challenges and hardships as those who were enslaved in the early parts of this republic. They want you to believe that reparations should be paid to those whose ancestors were brought here against their will. I've always had a problem with this way of thinking. I am white, a Caucasian, yet somehow I am automatically to blame for the sins of the past. The odd thing about this is that my ancestors had no slaves. They were fisherman in the Azores. As a matter of fact, they probably intermingled and associated with Africans along the Gold Coast. (Perhaps a DNA test is in order?) I do not see how I, or anyone else like me, should be forced to give up my hard-earned money to appease the guilty consciences of other people.

The concept that this nation is systemically racist is absurd and based on fever dreams.

Do racism and white supremacy exist? Yes, but not only in our country. Our enemies want us to focus on red herrings so we do not see the real danger of what they propose. They want to make and keep minorities victims so that they can further their own goals.

Society has become so decadent and disconnected from morality that things once thought unthinkable are out and open in public view. The media has advanced the sexualization of virtually everything and everyone, as has the entertainment industry. After all, sex sells, right? The problem is the age scale is sliding lower. And we are getting to the point where people are openly advocating that pedophilia is OK. That we should call pedophiles *minor-attracted people*. And changing the sex of a child without them having a brain capable of understanding the ramifications of what is being done to them is a cause to be celebrated. And then there are those who prey on the young and defenseless. We will probably never know all the names on Jeffrey Epstein's list, and that is because they are protecting themselves from the anger and ire of the people.

Now to accomplish what they want, some things have to change. First and foremost, the language. There are actual discussions as to whether or not a man who's had a sex change operation and turned himself into a woman is really a woman. Now do not get me wrong. The libertarian part of me has no problem with people making choices for themselves as long as they are consenting adults. I draw the line when decisions are made for children who do not fully under the choices being made for them.

Do you have a mother, or a birthing person? Sure, both describe the same basic thing, but one has a more far-reaching context that leftists want to eradicate. Men can be pregnant. Didn't you know that? The audacity and absurdity of these ludicrous statements appeal to those who want to change the way society exists. Words have meaning, unless you convince others that the meaning is flawed and should be replaced with another.

To those who would change the English language, I caution you on your approach, for it will only annoy and vindicate those whose minds you are trying to change. When someone says, "I identify as … …" …" it can be replaced by "I pretend to be … …" …" without changing the context. If I identify as a lion, is it a metaphorical or literal statement? The same reasoning can be applied to the fact that I am pretending to be a lion.

It is also easy to ridicule those who espouse the idea of toxic masculinity. They focus on all the bad and negative aspects of the male and dismiss those that are good, and even the parts of the *toxic* ones that are positive. It would seem the goal is to change the masculine into feminine, or at least soften it. Whether you are a man or a woman, each sex has its own specific positive and negative traits. Calling out the negative aspects of the masculine, while ignoring the ones of the feminine, seems to be counterproductive to a logical debate on the subject. Then again, the goal is not logical debate. It is the transformation and subjugation of what is seen as negative by those who push the agenda. I cannot help but wonder why this one-sided farce is allowed to continue in our society. Welcome to modern-day feminism.

Perhaps you have noticed that if you do

not follow the leftist agenda and align yourself with progressives you are automatically labeled a bigot, a racist, a sexist, or some sort of phobic person? Self-serving politicians pay lip service at the altar of wokeness and political correctness to advance their own causes. These so-called *representatives* do not do this for the public good. They do it for themselves.

The rabid and demented ministrations of the left have done nothing but act against this great republic. They wail and scream for diversity, inclusivity, and equity at the expense of the very system that gave them the gifts that allowed such thought. To what end do these left-leaning progressives champion their cause? What is the goal of socialism, or so-called democratic socialism? Or communism? Why disallow the logical, rational, and sane practice of discourse and disagreement? Why do they shout down and disregard those who do not adhere to their dogma?

To understand the propaganda, you must first buy into DIE: diversity, inclusivity, and equity.

Diversity is no substitute for ability. What good does it do to have a workforce that is diverse in skin color if you have members who clearly aren't the best candidates for the job? It reeks of the affirmative action that helped to devolve our education system. Give me the best of the best to do my work! I do not care about skin color, ethnicity, or creed. I care about results! MLK was so right. It is about the content of your character and nothing else.

Inclusivity is just as dangerous. Again, on the surface, the idea has some merit, but the methodology with which it is carried out leaves a lot to be desired. One of the most glaring examples of this is in the legal immigration system. I know many ethnically Portuguese people whose families came to the United States in the 1920s who have no idea about their original culture or language.

The original concept of the great American melting pot served this nation well. It was expected that if you wanted to participate in America, you would learn the language and customs, effectively abandoning what and where you came from. Fast-forward to the 1960s and the policy changed. The melting pot was replaced with the salad bowl and a celebration of ethnicity was the order of the day. Instead of forcing someone to learn the English language (which was not the official language of the republic but the de facto language), now we enable mediocrity by allowing people to keep their original languages and acquiescing to assist them in those languages. My home state actually publishes instructions for official documents in something like twenty-six languages. This system of inclusivity has resulted in an amalgam of the American language and culture that is quickly becoming a thing of the past.

One may ask, "What is wrong with this?" The problem is that rather than empowering people to become good citizens of the republic, it is enabling them to remain on the periphery of the society. The act of enabling someone has never been a positive way to accomplish anything. It is tantamount to appeasement, which is the lazy/cowardly way out of dealing with an issue. I invite those who champion this cause to attempt to emigrate to France and see if the French will indulge the same allowances. Or would they expect you to acquiesce and learn the language of the land?

There is a happy medium that should be pursued. There is nothing wrong with remembering the culture and traditions of your family's original country, or the language. However, this should not be imposed on someone or expected of them. It is incumbent upon each individual to decide for themselves whether or not to respect this practice. One can become a thriving and participating member of American society and still pay homage to their heritage. Perhaps the most glaring mistake the Founding Fathers made was not to make English the official language of the republic. It is time for this notion to be made into law, lest we continue to slide into mediocrity.

Equity does not compute to equality. It is equality of outcomes, which flies in the face of every standard of a free market economy. That means company A and company B make the same amount of money even if company A has better products, staff, and services. That is anathema to capitalism. Yes, capitalism produces inequality, but so does every economic system we have invented. The difference is that only free market capitalism has resulted in the production of wealth. At many levels, it has risen the impoverished out of their base levels of existence.

What we have is a bitter and exceedingly polarizing state of affairs in what seems to be a battle of wills over the soul of the republic. Whether you are left or right, liberal or conservative, you should be concerned at the agitated levels of behavior shown by everyone. Both sides will claim to be right, and both sides will claim to have the proper solutions. But the fact is that this nation has, for decades, socially, morally, and somewhat politically, been shifted toward the left. I say *somewhat* because there have been brief periods of interruption where it has shifted to the right. But overall, the axis of advance of our civilization is centered on leftist ideals. And anyone who knows their history of America will understand that this cannot stand. If you do not realize that, then you need to educate yourself. The words of the Founding Fathers are easily obtainable and easily read.

Was it truly necessary to have the level of property damage across the nation that occurred due to the (admittedly unnecessary) death of a career criminal? Organizations such as BLM claim to stand for something, yet those who created it are self-confessed, avowed Marxists who have ulterior motives. Then the unexpected outcome of an election in which there were questions that were not timely answered about integrity resulted in an *insurrection* at the capital of this nation. Add to this a poorly managed and mishandled pandemic response and you have ordinary citizens at each other's throat.

It should be noticed by everyone that the leftists love their labels. What I mean by that is that progressive thought drives on ascribing descriptive words to every category of person. It is a methodology that seeks to establish many small collectives rather than focus on each individual with their own merits. On a hypocritical note, the left will decry those who try to spread their religious beliefs to those who do not want them. Yet they are perfectly fine with the gender fluid pushing their beliefs on the population, even though some may not want it.

Chapter 6

The Fate of the American Republic

You may not agree with every thought I have written down, but hopefully you do see that the progressive, leftist, liberal agenda has done nothing positive for this nation and re-public in the last six decades in which it has been in overdrive. You are free to dismiss the parts you do not like and accept the parts you do. That is part of what living in a free society and being a free individual is all about. My in-tention was to introduce thoughts that would make you think and evaluate what has been happening in your own life and in the lives of your fellow people. These words may not be especially popular as this time in our society. However, they must be said, and they should be heard by everyone. Why? Because the free exchange of ideas is the only way in which we can overcome difficulties and obstacles and come together to a resolution that will make this republic great again.

The middle path is the best step forward to appease most of the population. That is to say, middle-of-the-road policies will be pop-ular with the majority of the people. Fringe element policies are never popular except with those on the fringes. Whether you are a moral Christian conservative or a fanatical leftist feminist, you must realize that your views are not held by the majority. It does not mean your views should be ignored or stamped out, but it does mean that decisions must be made in a prism that shed light on most of society.

Will this necessary and important change in our political and social systems occur? I certainly hope so, and I have done my best to lay the case for it. Will it require a revolution or civil war? The only thing I know is to follow Frederick Douglass's wisdom: fight for your rights at the ballot box, in the jury box, and if necessary, from the cartridge box. Challenge political candidates to determine whether or not they are constitutional conservatives. Challenge unlawful/unconstitutional laws in the courts. If enough of "We the People" do these two things, then the likelihood of needing the third option diminishes greatly.

Doing these things requires courage and conviction, values that are in severely short supply in our representatives. It is up to "We the People" to fight the good fight to institute change. Without the will to stand up for your natural rights, nothing will ever change.

Will our posterity continue to be subject to progressive and leftist indoctrination? There is a movement recently to take back the reigns of control over government as many parents in various school districts started, and continue to, challenge their school boards over aspects of their children's education. We can only hope that this individual, patriotic spirit will continue to catch fire in other aspects of our culture and society.

Will our society, our culture, and our nation survive the decades of relentless assault from the left, or will they fade into socialist obscurity, brought on by our own decadence? Will we once again enshrine the idea of the limited government to represent us? That is a question that can only be answered by you, the reader. Challenge the populist narrative and learn facts and truths for yourselves. Before it is too late, take back the republic!

> If anyone can show me, and
> prove to me, that I am wrong
> in thought or deed, I will gladly

change. I seek the truth, which never yet hurt anybody. It is only persistence in self-delusion and ignorance which does harm. (Marcus Aurelius)

9 781666 732956